Assalamu Alaykum,
my name is Qamar!

What's your name?

....

That's such a cool name!

This is your Ramadan Journal & Activity Book.

Your Ramadan, little Legacy, begins here!

Bismillah,
Let's go!

Welcome for Parents

Assalamu Alaykum Dear Parents & Carers,

May Allah reward you for the love and commitment you give in bringing up your children, every day.

The Ramadan Journal & Activity Book, is specially designed to take your child on an educational and interactive journey.

This journal will help your child to track their Ramadan progress, as well as complete a daily educational activity that is inspired by a Juz of the Qur'an. It's also cross-curricular, which means that it will help develop both their secular and Islamic studies at the same time.

Be sure to join in on the journey and support your child where needed!

رَبِّ هَبْ لِى مِنَ ٱلصَّٰلِحِين

"My Lord, grant me [a child] from among the righteous."
(37:100)

With du'as and peace
Towards Faith Kids Team

Welcome for Kids

Assalamu Alaykum Friends!

My name is Qamar and I am here to take you on an adventure! If you haven't guessed yet, I'm the moon in the sky. (Not a banana!)

I'm glad you've joined me. I need some help... I need to travel all the way back home, up into the sky, to tell everyone it is the day of Eid.

But before I do that, I need to find all of my coins that I lost from my knowledge bag. I can't go home without them!

Can you help me please?

Ah! I knew you would want to help! To collect the coins we need to complete a fun activity each day in Ramadan. I will also help you to keep track of your fasting, prayers and good deeds!

Bismillah, let's make an intention!

I .... intend

to have an awesome Ramadan and be the best I can be for Allah and my family!

What's Inside

Journal & Activity Book

Track your progress each day in Ramadan and complete the daily activities!

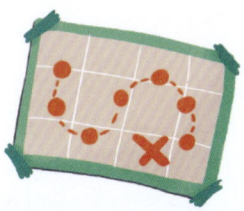

Activity Adventure Map

Put this up on your wall. Complete each daily activity and put a knowledge coin sticker on to the map!

Stickers

At the back of this book are all of your knowledge coin stickers and more stickers to track your Ramadan deeds.

Bookmark

Use the bookmark in this journal to track which day of Ramadan you are on.

How To Use

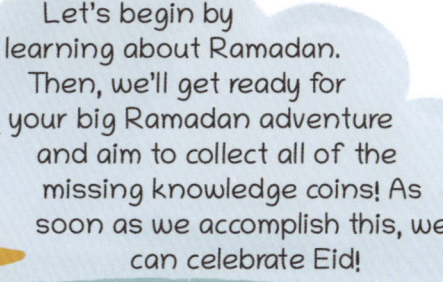

Let's begin by learning about Ramadan. Then, we'll get ready for your big Ramadan adventure and aim to collect all of the missing knowledge coins! As soon as we accomplish this, we can celebrate Eid!

Begin by Learning About Ramadan
Learn the secrets of Ramadan before we start.

Page No **7**

Prepare for Our Ramadan Adventure
Plan and prepare for Ramadan with exercises.

Page No **19**

Complete Our Ramadan Adventure Activities & Journal
Your daily Ramadan activities and track your Ramadan progress.

Page No **25**

Celebrate Eid
Finish with your Ramadan report card and celebrate Eid!

Page No **95**

Stage 1
Learning About Ramadan

Before we begin my friend, let's start with what Ramadan is!

Ramadan is...

The 4th Pillar of Islam

 Is the 9th month of the Islamic calendar

 A time to offer prayers

A time to ask for forgiveness

A time to do dhikr

 Going to the mosque to pray Taraweeh

 Fasting from sunrise to sunset

When the Qur'an was first revealed to the Prophet Muhammad (SAWS) on the night known as Laylat al-Qadr

 A time to learn, recite, and read Qur'an

 An opportunity to give charity

 A time to pay Zakat

 A time to be your best and earn extra reward from Allah

 EID AL FITR marks the end of Ramadan

The Adventure of Ramadan

My dear Ramadan travellers, let's start by learning a little bit about Ramadan. You will learn more about Ramadan through the daily activities we do too!

This month is the 9th month in the Islamic calendar, it's a little different to the calendar you normally follow at school.

The First Night of Ramadan

A new Islamic month begins when you see a new crescent moon in the sky (a crescent is just like the shape of a banana!). Guess what? That's me! As soon as someone spots me in the sky that means the month of Ramadan has begun. It's tricky to find me, because I'm great at playing hide and seek!

On the first night of Ramadan, you will notice something special. You will notice that people at home are rushing to the mosque to do a prayer called Taraweeh. Ask your family what Taraweeh is!

Ramadan Is The Month of Fasting

There's something else that you will begin to notice in Ramadan and that is that people in your home will begin to eat at night and not through the day. It's not because they are hungry or that they're eating snacks and chocolate at night, although sometimes they are! It's because, when Ramadan arrives we also begin to fast through the day. Fasting is to not eat or drink anything from the time of Fajr (sunrise) to Maghrib (sunset).

At the start of each day, before Fajr which is just before the sun rises, we make our intention to fast the next day. This is after eating food that will give us energy for the day. We call this meal 'Suhoor.'

At the end of each day, at Maghrib, when the sun sets, we have another meal to end our fast, as Allah doesn't want us to be hungry for so long. This is called Iftaar.

Ramadan Is A Pillar of Islam

Ramadan is the fourth pillar of Islam, which is when a lot of people fast during this month. Fasting is called 'Sawm' in Arabic. Can you say the word 'Sawm'? It has such an interesting sound right!

All adults need to fast in Ramadan. If you are sick, old, travelling or a child then you don't need to fast.

But, as I'm your dear friend Qamar, I want to train you up for Ramadan, so when you do become an adult, Insha'Allah, you are already a superhero at fasting during Ramadan!

Ramadan Is The Month of Rewards

In this special month, Muslims all around the world do as many prayers as they can, they read as much Qur'an as they can and do lots of good deeds. We already get a lot of rewards for the good deeds we do for Allah. But, during Ramadan, we get lots, lots more! It's a power-boost for all of the good deeds we do!

Ramadan is about being the best person we can be, which means working even harder on showing our best actions and manners at all times!

Ramadan Is The Month of The Qur'an

Did you know that the Qur'an was revealed to our Prophet Muhammad, peace be upon Him, in the month of Ramadan?

The Qur'an was brought down from a special place in the heavens, by a special angel called Jibreel (as) to our special Prophet Muhammad.

How cool is that! It was revealed on a special night called the 'Night of Power' (Laylat al-Qadr). We will learn more about this later!

Ramadan Riddles
Test Your Knowledge!

I was revealed in the month of Ramadan. Leave me and you will never find the treasure of happiness. I come in the form of words or the shape of a book. What am I?

I am the fourth pillar of Islam. I come once a year. I arrive and leave depending on the moon. What am I?

I am an important meal when the fast comes to an end but not when the fast begins. What am I?

I am the night the Qur'an was sent down. I am better than a thousand years. What am I?

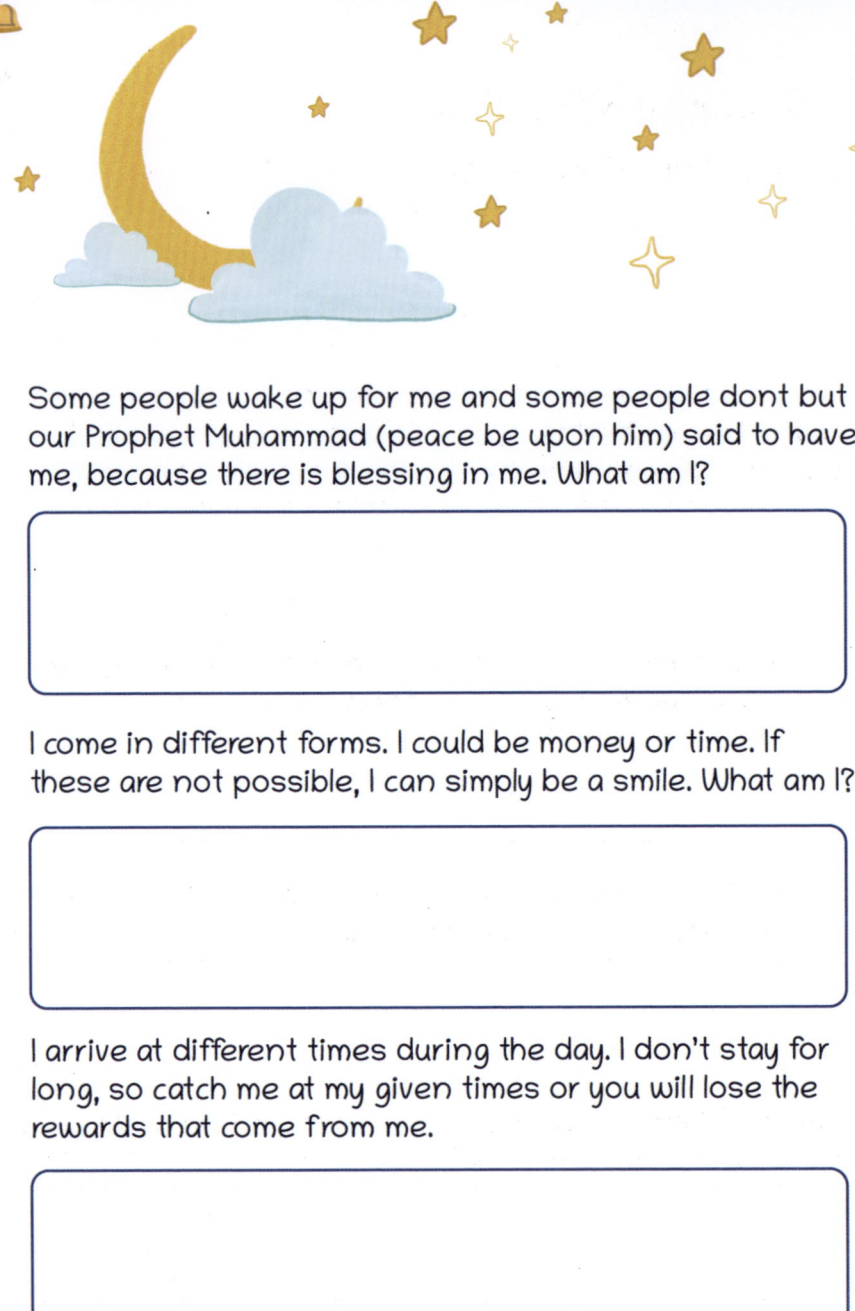

Some people wake up for me and some people dont but our Prophet Muhammad (peace be upon him) said to have me, because there is blessing in me. What am I?

I come in different forms. I could be money or time. If these are not possible, I can simply be a smile. What am I?

I arrive at different times during the day. I don't stay for long, so catch me at my given times or you will lose the rewards that come from me.

Ramadan Du'as

A du'a is a special request, like a wish, that we make to Allah. Throughout Ramadan there are different du'as you can make. You will find these du'as below and you can look back here to read them when needed!

For breaking your fast

ذَهَبَ الظَّمَأُ ، وَابْتَلَّتِ الْعُرُوقُ ، وَثَبَتَ الأَجْرُ إِنْ شَاءَ اللهُ

Transliteration
Dhahabadh-dhama', wabtillatil 'urooq, wa thabatal ajru inshaa'Allah

Translation
The thirst is gone, the veins are moistened, and the reward is certain if Allah wills.

On the last odd nights of Ramadan (Laylatul Qadr)

اللّهُمَّ إِنَّكَ عَفُوٌّ تُحِبُّ الْعَفْوَ فَاعْفُعَنِّي

Transliteration
Allahumma innaka afuwwun tuhibbu al-afwa fa'fu anni.

Translation
Oh Allah you are forgiving, and you love forgiveness, so forgive me.

Before Going to Sleep

بِاسْمِكَ اللَّهُمَّ أَمُوتُ وَأَحْيَاَ

Transliteration
Bismika allahumma amutu wa ahya.

Translation
In Your name, O Allah, I die and I live.

After Waking Up

الْحَمْدُ اللهِ الَّذِي أَحْيَانَا بَعْدَمَا أَمَاتَنَا وَإِلَيْهِ النُّشُور

Transliteration
Alhamdu lillaahil lathee 'ahyaanaa ba'da maa 'amaatanaa wa'ilayhin nushoor.

Translation
All praise is for Allah who gave us life after causing us to die, and unto him is the resurrection.

For Success In This Life & The Next Life

رَبَّنَآ ءَاتِنَا فِى ٱلدُّنْيَا حَسَنَةً وَفِى ٱلْأَخِرَةِ حَسَنَةً وَقِنَا عَذَابَ ٱلنَّارِ

Transliteration
Rabbanaaa aatinaa fid-dunyaa hasanatan wa fil-aakhirati hasanatan wa qinaa 'adhaaban-naar.

Translation
Our Lord! Give us in this world good and in the Hereafter good, and save us from the torment of the Fire.

For Thanking Parents

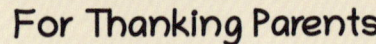

Transliteration
Rabban-aghfir lee wa liwaalidayya wa lilmu'mineena yawma yaqoom-ul-hisaab.

Translation
Our Lord! Forgive me and my parents, and (all) the believers on the Day when the reckoning will be established.

Stage 2
Preparing for Your Ramadan Adventure

Our planning and preparing for our Ramadan adventure starts here!

Before we begin our awesome adventure,

We need to prepare for Ramadan by being grateful for what we already have and planning ahead on what we want to do in Ramadan!

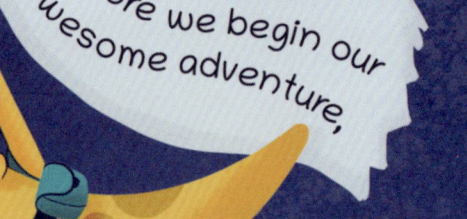

My friend don't forget that before we start our Ramadan adventure, you need to also put your Activity Adventure Map up on your wall!

Exercise 1

What are you happy about that Allah has given you?

Being grateful to Allah, means to appreciate everything that He has blessed us with, such as a home, family and good health. When we are grateful, Allah gets very happy and wants to give us more and more! Write or draw all of the things Allah has given you that you are thankful for. Think about the people in your life and the things you have.

Exercise 2

To do and not to do!

Complete the list of things you wish to do in Ramadan and the things you need to avoid. Islam teaches us to do as many good deeds as we can, but also to avoid doing anything that upsets or harms others. The more good deeds you do the more Allah will be happy with you.

Do's

Listening to family members

Doing my prayers

Reading Qur'an

_____

_____

_____

_____

_____

_____

Dont's

Disturbing others

Arguing

Telling lies

_____

_____

_____

_____

_____

_____

Exercise 3

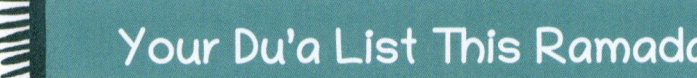

Your Du'a List This Ramadan

Your du'as are all the wishes you want to make to Allah.

The du'as that you make to Allah are like superpowers! When we make du'a to Allah, He listens to us and responds to us in the best way possible. All you need to do is raise your hands and ask Him!

Write down everything you wish from Allah this Ramadan! You can think about your health, your family, your school grades and even your Eid presents!

Kindness Chart

My little friend! In Ramadan, we get extra bonus reward points for every good deed we do! Try and do one good deed a day from the boxes below. Once you have completed a deed, colour in the box. By the end of Ramadan this should look very colourful, Insha'Allah!

Help prepare the table for iftar	Give salaam to as many people as you can	Hold the door for someone	Let someone else go in front of you in a line or queue	Lay the prayer mats out for a family member
Give your neighbour a card saying 'Ramadan Mubarak'	Take a glass of water for someone praying taraweeh	Pick up litter from the floor	Play with someone who looks lonely at school or at home	Tell a member of your family you love them for the sake of Allah
Make a du'a for people around the world	Give someone a warm smile	Feed the birds outside your home or the local park	Help your family with a chore around the house	Do dhikr of Allah with your family
Make a 'thank you' card for your teacher	Share a toy with someone	Ask your teacher how their day has been	Call a family member and ask how they are	Help clean the table after iftar
Learn a sunnah of the Prophet	Learn a du'a from the du'a page	Spend some time with an elderly person	Make an Eid card for someone special	Donate a toy or some money to charity
Recycle three items	Tidy your room and surprise your parents/carers	Say 'I love you' to someone else in your family	Learn a surah from the last chapter of the Qur'an	Thank your parents for 3 things

Stage 3
Your Ramadan Adventure Activities & Journal

Complete your daily Ramadan activities and record your Ramadan progress with stickers, colouring and writing!

Our big Ramadan adventure begins!

Help me find and collect all of the missing knowledge coins by completing the daily activities.

When you complete the daily activity look for the knowledge coin sticker at the back of this book. Stick this onto your Activity Adventure Map!

Also, we need to track what we are doing in each day in Ramadan, like our fasting and prayers. Use the stickers or grab a pen or pencil to mark what you've completed!

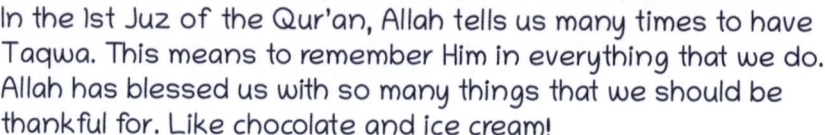

Day 1 Activity: Gratitude
1st Juz of The Qur'an

In the 1st Juz of the Qur'an, Allah tells us many times to have Taqwa. This means to remember Him in everything that we do. Allah has blessed us with so many things that we should be thankful for. Like chocolate and ice cream!

We can remember Allah at all times by thinking about what he has given us.

Fill this page up with as many of Allah's blessings you can think of. Think about your family and things you have at home. Write or draw in the space below.

Did you learn anything new about remembering Allah that you didn't know before?

....

Day 2 Activity: Fasting
2nd Juz of The Qur'an

When you are fasting there are so many rules to follow! Allah tells us the important rules about fasting in the Qur'an. He says, "Oh you who believe! Fasting is prescribed to you as it was prescribed to those before you, so that you may attain taqwa." (2:183).

Ask your friends and family about fasting and write down five important rules about fasting.

1. ....
....

2. ....
....

3. ....
....

4. ....
....

5. ....
....

Did you learn anything new about fasting that you didn't know before?

....

RAMADAN DAY 2

Date : ....

Salah

| Fajr | Dhuhr | Asr | Maghrib | Isha | Extra Prayers |

Fasting

- 1/4 Fast
- 1/2 Fast
- 3/4 Fast
- Full Fast!

Worship

- [ ] I read or learned Qur'an today
- [ ] I did a good deed on the kindness chart
- [ ] ....

How was your day?

Day 3 Activity: Protection
3rd Juz of The Qur'an

The 3rd Juz of the Qur'an has the most powerful verse in the entire Qur'an, known as 'Ayat al-Kursi'. If we recite these verses every day during fajr and 'asr time (and before sleeping if we can), we will be protected from bad things that can harm us. Think of it as a magnificent shield that can make these bad things run far, far away!

Read Ayat al-Kursi below and try to learn it throughout Ramadan.

اللَّهُ لَا إِلَٰهَ إِلَّا هُوَ الْحَيُّ الْقَيُّومُ

لَا تَأْخُذُهُ سِنَةٌ وَلَا نَوْمٌ

لَّهُ مَا فِي السَّمَاوَاتِ وَمَا فِي الْأَرْضِ

مَن ذَا الَّذِي يَشْفَعُ عِندَهُ إِلَّا بِإِذْنِهِ

يَعْلَمُ مَا بَيْنَ أَيْدِيهِمْ وَمَا خَلْفَهُمْ

وَلَا يُحِيطُونَ بِشَيْءٍ مِّنْ عِلْمِهِ إِلَّا بِمَا شَاءَ

وَسِعَ كُرْسِيُّهُ السَّمَاوَاتِ وَالْأَرْضَ

وَلَا يَئُودُهُ حِفْظُهُمَا وَهُوَ الْعَلِيُّ الْعَظِيمُ

Find out from your family or friends where exactly this verse is in the Qur'an and write it down below!

....

RAMADAN DAY 3

Date : ....

Salah

| Fajr | Dhuhr | Asr | Maghrib | Isha | Extra Prayers |

Fasting

- 1/4 Fast
- 1/2 Fast
- 3/4 Fast
- Full Fast!

Worship

- [ ] I read or learned Qur'an today
- [ ] I did a good deed on the kindness chart
- [ ] ....

....

How was your day?

Day 4 Activity: Du'a
4th Juz of The Qur'an

Let me tell you the story of Prophet Zakariyya (peace be upon him). He made du'a to Allah to grant him good children. This is important because it teaches us that we should make du'a for our future before it even happens. As mentioned earlier, a du'a is like a wish, something you ask Allah for, which you really want in your life.

Make a list of du'as for each of the sections below.

Family	Friends	Poorer People Around The World

School	Activities	Anything Else!

Did you know? When you raise your hands to make du'a, Allah feels shy to leave your hands empty. This means Allah answers our du'as, we just have to ask!

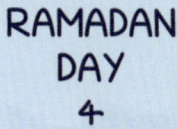

RAMADAN DAY 4

Date : ....

Salah

| Fajr | Dhuhr | Asr | Maghrib | Isha | Extra Prayers |

Fasting

- 1/4 Fast
- 1/2 Fast
- 3/4 Fast
- Full Fast!

Worship

- ☐ I read or learned Qur'an today
- ☐ I did a good deed on the kindness chart
- ☐ ....

....

How was your day?

Day 5 Activity: Fairness
5th Juz of The Qur'an

In the 5th Juz of the Qur'an, Allah teaches us to be fair all the time. That basically means we shouldn't be a meany! :)

Read the stories below and colour the faces if you think the story is fair or unfair.

Musa was playing with play dough for a long time. Ibrahim came over to the table to play with the play dough too. Musa continued to play and Ibrahim watched.	 Fair / Unfair
Fatima is riding a bike for 30 minutes. Hanaa comes and asks if she can have a turn. Fatima says "no" every time and continues to ride the bike.	 Fair / Unfair
Yahya was having a party for completing the Qur'an. He invited everyone from his class to come to the party.	 Fair / Unfair

Pick one of the situations from above that is unfair. What could you do to make it fair? Think about what you can say or do to make things better.

....

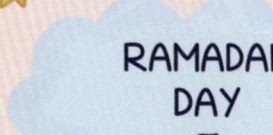

RAMADAN DAY 5

Date : ....

Salah

| Fajr | Dhuhr | Asr | Maghrib | Isha | Extra Prayers |

Fasting

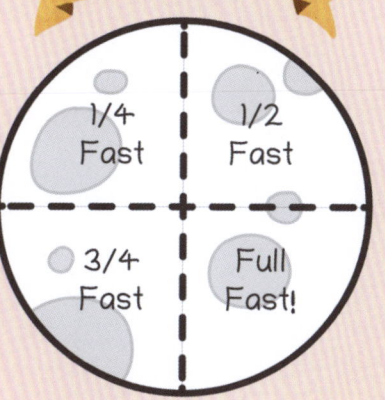

1/4 Fast | 1/2 Fast | 3/4 Fast | Full Fast!

Worship

- [ ] I read or learned Qur'an today
- [ ] I did a good deed on the kindness chart
- [ ] ....

....

How was your day?

Day 6 Activity: Wudu
6th Juz of The Qur'an

In the 6th Juz of the Qur'an, Allah tells us about doing wudu before our prayer. Very carefully, watch a member of your family perform wudu. Draw and write down all the steps of wudu in the boxes below. Remember to write the steps in order.

Step 1

Step 2

Step 3

Step 4

Step 5

Step 6

Step 7

Step 8

Masha'Allah! You know how to perform wudu. Now try to teach it to someone at home without looking at your drawings!

Day 7 Activity: Miracles
7th Juz of The Qur'an

My friend, do you know what a 'miracle' is? It is when Allah makes enormous, special things happen to special people! In the Qur'an, we learn about Prophet Isa (as), who is also known as 'Jesus'. Did you know, Allah allowed Isa (as) to make miracles happen too!

In the shapes below colour in the miracles that Isa (as) had performed. You may need some help from people at home to get the right answer.

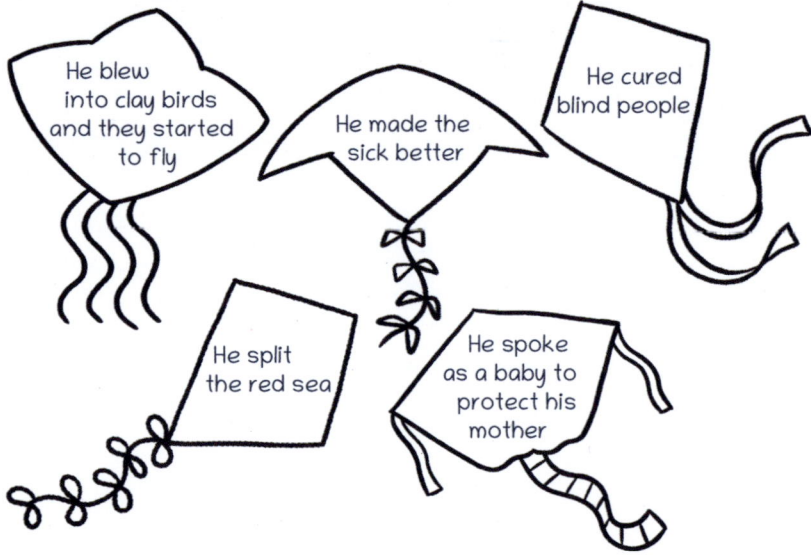

- He blew into clay birds and they started to fly
- He made the sick better
- He cured blind people
- He split the red sea
- He spoke as a baby to protect his mother

These miracles happened only with the permission of Allah. Can you find out which Prophet the other miracles were given to?

....

RAMADAN DAY 7

Date : ....

Salah

| Fajr | Dhuhr | Asr | Maghrib | Isha | Extra Prayers |

Fasting

- 1/4 Fast
- 1/2 Fast
- 3/4 Fast
- Full Fast!

Worship

- ☐ I read or learned Qur'an today
- ☐ I did a good deed on the kindness chart
- ☐ ....
  ....

How was your day?

Day 8 Activity: The Creation
8th Juz of The Qur'an

In the 8th Juz of the Qur'an, Allah tells us the story of the first man that was ever created. His name was Adam (as).

In the story below, fill in the missing blanks with the words given. If it gets tricky, you can always ask someone to help you!

ADAM - ANGELS - IBLIS - HAWA
FORBIDDEN - EARTH - MERCIFUL

Allah created .... and ordered the .... to bow down to him.
.... did not bow down to Adam. Iblis became a disbeliever and promised to trick people. Allah then created .... and told her and Adam to eat the fruits around them, except from one tree. Iblis tricked them. He told them if they eat from the .... tree they would live forever. Adam and Hawa disobeyed Allah by eating from that tree. Allah sent them out of Jannah to live on ....

Adam and Hawa cried so much and kept asking Allah for forgiveness. Because Allah is .... and forgiving, He forgave them.

What are the names of the first two son's of Adam (as)?
....

RAMADAN DAY 8

Date : ....

Salah

| Fajr | Dhuhr | Asr | Maghrib | Isha | Extra Prayers |

Fasting

- 1/4 Fast
- 1/2 Fast
- 3/4 Fast
- Full Fast!

Worship

- [ ] I read or learned Qur'an today
- [ ] I did a good deed on the kindness chart
- [ ] ....

....

How was your day?

Day 9 Activity: Patience
9th Juz of The Qur'an

In the 9th Juz of the Qur'an we learn about the beautiful story of Musa (as). Musa, also known as Moses, was a Prophet who was a superhero for children! The children of Israel were going through a difficult time living under the rule of a very bad ruler, called Firoun, who was a Pharaoh. He was very mean to them and made them work as slaves. My fellow travellers, how would you feel if someone made you work all day and never gave you a break? Musa saved all of the children and taught the children how to be patient and how to look to Allah for strength, when the Pharaoh was giving them a tough time!

Write about a time where you had to be really patient. For example, when someone had hurt your feelings or you were going through any other difficult times.

What dua would you make to Allah to make these hard times easier for you?

....

RAMADAN DAY 9

Date : ....

Salah

| Fajr | Dhuhr | Asr | Maghrib | Isha | Extra Prayers |

Fasting

- 1/4 Fast
- 1/2 Fast
- 3/4 Fast
- Full Fast!

Worship

- ☐ I read or learned Qur'an today
- ☐ I did a good deed on the kindness chart
- ☐ ....

How was your day?

Day 10 Activity: Islamic Months
10th Juz of The Qur'an

In the 10th Juz of the Qur'an, Allah tells us about the months in the Islamic calendar. This is different to the calendar you will see at school. The Islamic calendar is based on the moon and the normal gregorian calendar is based on the sun. Complete the names of the Islamic months below. Ask the people at home for help to research online.

M _ _ _ _ r _ _   R _ _ a _

S _ _ a _   S _ _ ' _ a _

R _ _ _ _ l - _ _ _ _ _   R _ _ _ _ _ a _

R _ _ _ A _ _ - _ _ _ _ _   S _ _ _ _ a _

J _ _ _ _ _ _ A _ - _ _ _ _ _   D _ _ ' _ - Q _ ' _ _ _

J _ _ _ _ _ A _ _ - _ _ _ _ _   D _ _ _ - H _ _ _ _

Find the four sacred months and match them with the correct description

M.....................O   O This is the month where the Prophet (saw) made the night journey from the kaaba to Al aqsa and then to the heavens.

R.....................O   O This is the first month of the Islamic new year and ashura is on the 10th day of this month.

D.....................O   O This is the eleventh month of the Islamic calendar and comes before the month of Hajj.

D.....................O   O This is the month where muslims do hajj and celebrate Eid ul Adha

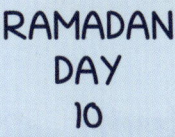

RAMADAN DAY 10

Date : ....

Salah

| Fajr | Dhuhr | Asr | Maghrib | Isha | Extra Prayers |

Fasting

- 1/4 Fast
- 1/2 Fast
- 3/4 Fast
- Full Fast!

Worship

☐ I read or learned Qur'an today

☐ I did a good deed on the kindness chart

☐ ....

....

How was your day?

Day 1-10 Reflection Page

Let's take a break! How's it going so far?

Alhamdulillah! We have completed the first 10 days of Ramadan! We have learnt so much already and I am really excited to learn more with you.

What have you learnt so far?
....
....

What did you enjoy doing the most?
....
....

What did you least enjoy?
....
....

What was your best deed or action so far?
....
....

What can you do to make your next 10 days of Ramadan better?
....
....

Day 11 Activity: Mistakes
11th Juz of The Qur'an

In the 11th Juz of the Qur'an, Allah tells us about Prophet Yunus (as). My fellow travellers, Prophet Yunus was swallowed by a whale, but through making du'a to Allah he managed to get out! Prophet Yunus was trying to convince a group of people to become Muslim and remember Allah but he became impatient, angry and left them! Because of this, Allah wanted the Prophet Yunus to reflect on this behaviour.

Number the sentences from 1 to 7 in the correct order of the story. You may ask others to help you or research the story online.

- [ ] A whale swallows Prophet Yunus, where he reads a du'a for forgiveness.
- [ ] Yunus (as) sets sail on a boat.
- [ ] The people of Nineveh are really happy to see Yunus (as) again.
- [ ] Yunus (as) tells the people to believe in Allah alone.
- [ ] A storm came and the people on the boat selected Yunus (as) to jump into the sea as part of their strange traditions.
- [ ] Yunus (as) left his people in anger.
- [ ] The people of Nineveh reject his call to worship Allah only.

What was the special du'a Yunus (as) made for forgiveness, when he was in the belly of the whale? Write it in Arabic or English.

....

RAMADAN DAY 11

Date : ....

Salah

Fajr | Dhuhr | Asr | Maghrib | Isha | Extra Prayers

Fasting

- 1/4 Fast
- 1/2 Fast
- 3/4 Fast
- Full Fast!

Worship

- [ ] I read or learned Qur'an today
- [ ] I did a good deed on the kindness chart
- [ ] ....

....

How was your day?

Day 12 Activity: Yusuf
12th Juz of The Qur'an

In the 12th Juz of the Qur'an, we learn the story of Yusuf (as).

Find out 4 facts about the story of Yusuf (as) and write them down in the buckets below. Then, colour in the well. You may need help from people at home to research the story.

Did you know? Yusuf and his father had a really special bond. Yusuf (as) called his father 'abati', which means 'beloved father' and his father called him 'bunaiya', which means 'beloved son'.

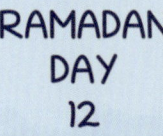

RAMADAN DAY 12

Date : ....

Salah

| Fajr | Dhuhr | Asr | Maghrib | Isha | Extra Prayers |

Fasting

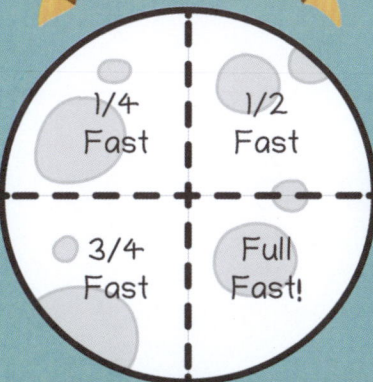

- 1/4 Fast
- 1/2 Fast
- 3/4 Fast
- Full Fast!

Worship

- [ ] I read or learned Qur'an today
- [ ] I did a good deed on the kindness chart
- [ ] ....
- ....

How was your day?

Day 13 Activity: Allah's Help
13th Juz of The Qur'an

Allah tells us about Prophet Ibrahim (as) in the 13th Juz of the Qur'an. Let's see if you can find out more about his amazing story by doing your own research online or by asking others. Then, try answering the questions below. For each question, tick one correct answer.

Why did the people around Prophet Ibrahim pray to idols?
☐ They thought the stones could talk
☐ They fell for Shaytan's trick
☐ They liked the way the idols looked

Prophet Ibrahim had a plan to get rid of the idols and so when the people around him left, what did he do to the idols?
☐ He threw them into a river
☐ He hid them in a tent
☐ He smashed all of the idols

Why did the people around Prophet Ibrahim want to hurt him?
☐ They thought he was a danger to how they wanted to live
☐ They wanted to show how strong they are
☐ They didn't like the type of food he ate

The people around Prophet Ibrahim threw him into a fire, why did the fire not hurt him?
☐ It began to rain and the fire was put out
☐ The fire was not hot enough
☐ Allah told the fire to be cool for him

Why do you think Allah helped the Prophet Ibrahim when he was thrown into a fire?

....

RAMADAN DAY 13

Date : ....

Salah

- Fajr
- Dhuhr
- Asr
- Maghrib
- Isha
- Extra Prayers

Fasting

- 1/4 Fast
- 1/2 Fast
- 3/4 Fast
- Full Fast!

Worship

- [ ] I read or learned Qur'an today
- [ ] I did a good deed on the kindness chart
- [ ] ....

How was your day?

Day 14 Activity: Nature
14th Juz of The Qur'an

Let me tell you something fascinating! Von-Frisch won a Nobel prize in 1973 for his research on the behaviour of bees. He found that when a bee discovers a new flower, it would go back and tell the other bees the direction to get there. This is called a 'bee dance'. Sounds quite funny, doesn't it! But, did you know that Allah had already written this miracle in the 14th Juz of the Qur'an. Allah says, "...the Lord taught the bee to build its cells in hills, on trees...eat of all the produce, and find with skill and spacious paths of its lord". (Al-Qur'an 16:68-69) .

Help the bees untangle their way to their flowers. Use a different colour for each flower.

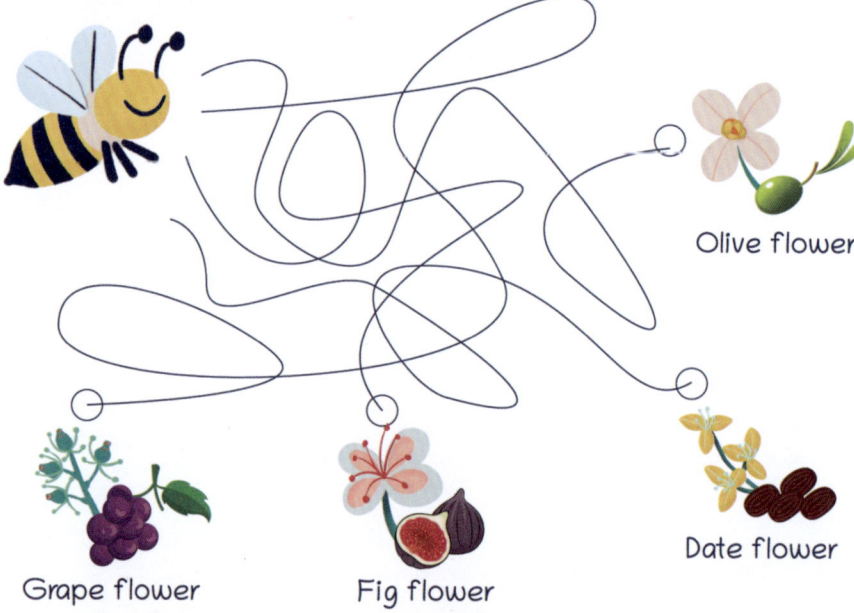

Did you know all of these fruits are also mentioned in the Qur'an?

RAMADAN DAY 14

Date : ....

Salah

| Fajr | Dhuhr | Asr | Maghrib | Isha | Extra Prayers |

Fasting

- 1/4 Fast
- 1/2 Fast
- 3/4 Fast
- Full Fast!

Worship

- [ ] I read or learned Qur'an today
- [ ] I did a good deed on the kindness chart
- [ ] ....

....

How was your day?

Day 15 Activity: Insha'Allah
15th Juz of The Qur'an

In the 15th Juz of the Qur'an, Allah tells us to say Insha'Allah, when we are planning to do something. For example, "Insha'Allah, I will go to school next week."

We don't say Insha'Allah for something that is already happening or has happened. For example, if someone asked you what are you doing? You wouldn't say I am eating insha'Allah.

Colour in all the boxes with the statements, where you would say Insha'Allah.

I am going to build a cardboard mosque	My name is Fatima	I will go to my grandparents house next week	I am fasting today
Tomorrow, I will recite Qur'an	I will pray all my Salahs today	I had a great time playing outside	I recited Qur'an today

Allah also tells us that if we forget to say 'insha'Allah' when we plan to do something or 'Bismillah' when we start something, then we should say it as soon as we remember!

RAMADAN DAY 15

Date : ....

Salah

| Fajr | Dhuhr | Asr | Maghrib | Isha | Extra Prayers |

Fasting

- 1/4 Fast
- 1/2 Fast
- 3/4 Fast
- Full Fast!

Worship

- [ ] I read or learned Qur'an today
- [ ] I did a good deed on the kindness chart
- [ ] ....

How was your day?

Day 16 Activity: Provisions
16th Juz of The Qur'an

Allah tells us about the story of Maryam (as). Maryam was given the blessing of having a baby called Isa (as) who is also known as Jesus, as mentioned before. One day, Maryam (as) sat next to a flowing stream, under a tree of dates.

Allah then told Maryam to eat the dates and drink the water. Find the tree full of dates in the picture below.

What are the benefits of eating dates? Find out and write down the answer below!

....

RAMADAN DAY 16

Date : ....

Salah

- Fajr
- Dhuhr
- Asr
- Maghrib
- Isha
- Extra Prayers

Fasting

- 1/4 Fast
- 1/2 Fast
- 3/4 Fast
- Full Fast!

Worship

- I read or learned Qur'an today ☐
- I did a good deed on the kindness chart ☐
- .... ☐

How was your day?

 ☐
 ☐
 ☐

Day 17 Activity: Hajj
17th Juz of The Qur'an

Hey Ramadan traveller! Have you ever seen a picture of the Ka'ba? It's the big black box you see with lots of Muslims around it! In the 17th Juz of the Qur'an, Allah tells us about the pilgrimage, Hajj. Hajj is a blessed journey wherein Muslims perform lots of good deeds. One of these good deeds is visiting the Ka'ba. You might have heard this being called 'the House of Allah.' But of course, Allah doesn't live in there!

Draw the Ka'ba in the space below and colour it in. Can you name the shape? How many sides, faces and vertices does this shape have?

Do you know who built the Ka'bah? Find out the answer and write it down in the space below!

....

RAMADAN DAY 17

Date : ....

Salah

| Fajr | Dhuhr | Asr | Maghrib | Isha | Extra Prayers |

Fasting

- 1/4 Fast
- 1/2 Fast
- 3/4 Fast
- Full Fast!

Worship

- [ ] I read or learned Qur'an today
- [ ] I did a good deed on the kindness chart
- [ ] ....

....

How was your day?

Day 18 Activity: Nuh (as)
18th Juz of The Qur'an

Let me tell you the story of Nuh (as), also known as Noah, and his massive boat which was called an Ark. In the 18th Juz of the Qur'an, Allah tells Prophet Nuh to build a big boat because there was a huge flood approaching. He then told him to take two of each type of animal and all the good people onto the boat to save them from drowning in the flood!

We have another fun activity today. Colour in the picture below and answer our reflective questions too!

Can you think of a time when you helped or saved someone else from being hurt?

....

RAMADAN DAY 18

Date : ....

Salah

- Fajr
- Dhuhr
- Asr
- Maghrib
- Isha
- Extra Prayers

Fasting

- 1/4 Fast
- 1/2 Fast
- 3/4 Fast
- Full Fast!

Worship

- [ ] I read or learned Qur'an today
- [ ] I did a good deed on the kindness chart
- [ ] ....

How was your day?

Day 19 Activity: Musa
19th Juz of The Qur'an

In the 19th Juz of the Qur'an, Allah tells us a great story of Prophet Musa (as) who is also known as 'Moses' in English. Prophet Musa (as) was saving a group of people, including children, from a really bad ruler called Firoun. When he was running away from Firoun with all of the children he was stuck. In front of him was a large, deep sea! Prophet Musa (as) had a special staff and he whacked it onto the ground. The sea then split into two! It was Allah who inspired Musa (as) to whack his staff onto the ground to make this happen. Musa (as) then crossed the sea with the group of people he saved. Alhamdullilah!

Can you think of a time when someone saved you from a difficult situation? Write it down in the space below.

We still remember the day when Musa (as) and his people were saved from Firoun? What is the name of this special day, and what do Muslims do?

RAMADAN DAY 19

Date : ....

Salah

| Fajr | Dhuhr | Asr | Maghrib | Isha | Extra Prayers |

Fasting

- 1/4 Fast
- 1/2 Fast
- 3/4 Fast
- Full Fast!

Worship

- [ ] I read or learned Qur'an today
- [ ] I did a good deed on the kindness chart
- [ ] ....

How was your day?

Day 20 Activity: Allah's Protection
20th Juz of The Qur'an

My fellow travellers! Can you imagine a little baby placed into a basket and then that basket placed into a river? What do you think would happen to the basket? Will the baby be safe? Let me tell you the story of Prophet Musa (as). When he was born, his life was in danger as the evil ruler Firoun wanted to hurt all new born boys. So, Musa's (as)'s mother hid him in a basket and then placed him into a river so no-one could find him. She did this as Allah told her to do so.

Let's see if you can help baby Musa find his way to the pharaoh's palace.

Can you think of a time when someone had protected you. What did they do and did you say thank you to them?

RAMADAN DAY 20

Date : ....

Salah

- Fajr
- Dhuhr
- Asr
- Maghrib
- Isha
- Extra Prayers

Fasting

- 1/4 Fast
- 1/2 Fast
- 3/4 Fast
- Full Fast!

Worship

- I read or learned Qur'an today ☐
- I did a good deed on the kindness chart ☐
- .... ☐

How was your day?

Day 11-20 Reflection Page

Let's take a break! How's it going so far?

Alhamdulillah! We have completed the second 10 days of Ramadan! We have learnt so much already and I am really excited to learn more with you.

What have you learnt so far?
....
....

What did you enjoy doing the most?
....
....

What did you least enjoy?
....
....

What was your best deed or action so far?
....
....

What can you do to make your next 10 days of Ramadan better?
....
....

Day 21 Activity: Praying
21st Juz of The Qur'an

Praying! Yep! This is the beautiful action we perform throughout the day to worship and bow down to Allah. In the 21st Juz of the Qur'an, Allah tells us that those who pray their prayers and give charity will be successful. Isn't this amazing!

There are 5 different prayers that we must pray each day. Draw in the clock hands for the salah times today.

Time to pray!

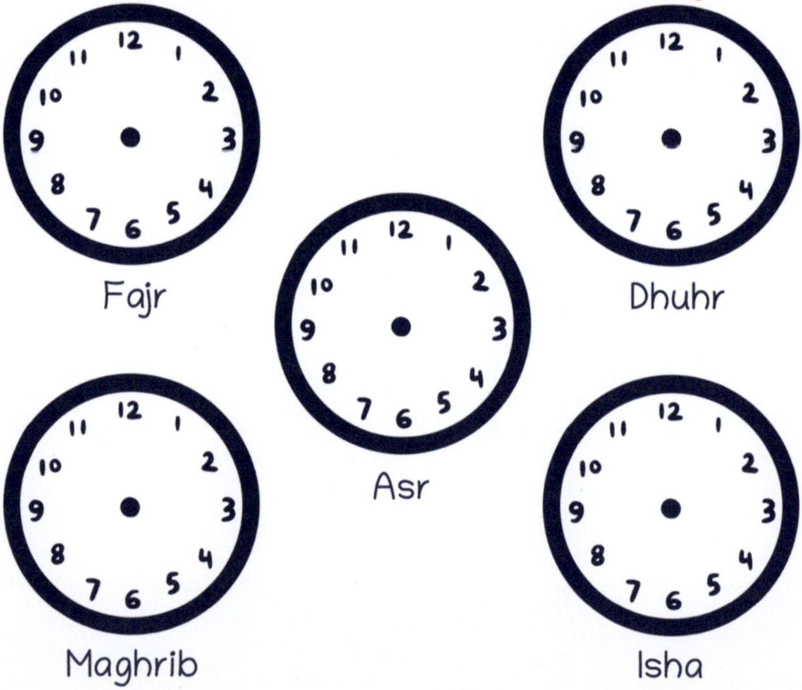

Fajr

Dhuhr

Asr

Maghrib

Isha

RAMADAN DAY 21

Date : ....

Salah

| Fajr | Dhuhr | Asr | Maghrib | Isha | Extra Prayers |

Fasting

- 1/4 Fast
- 1/2 Fast
- 3/4 Fast
- Full Fast!

Worship

I read or learned Qur'an today ☐

I did a good deed on the kindness chart ☐

.... ☐

....

How was your day?

Day 22 Activity: Nature
22nd Juz of The Qur'an

In the 22nd Juz of the Qur'an, Allah tells us about some of his beautiful creations. He tells us there are two types of water in the sea. One is sweet, fresh water and the other is bitter and salty. We eat fish from both types of waters. Can you remember the last time you ate fish? Maybe some yummy fish fingers?

With the help of people at home and your own research, draw different types of fish that live in freshwater and ones that live in saltwater below!

Freshwater Fish

Saltwater Fish

RAMADAN DAY 22

Date : ....

Salah

| Fajr | Dhuhr | Asr | Maghrib | Isha | Extra Prayers |

Fasting

- 1/4 Fast
- 1/2 Fast
- 3/4 Fast
- Full Fast!

Worship

- [ ] I read or learned Qur'an today
- [ ] I did a good deed on the kindness chart
- [ ] ....
- ....

How was your day?

Day 23 Activity: The Heart
23rd Juz of The Qur'an

In the 23rd Juz of the Qur'an, we come across the remarkable Surah Yaseen. This surah is known as the heart of the Qur'an. Did you know, our bodies have many organs, but the most important one is the heart. When the heart is warm, the body is alive and working. Your heart guides you in life and it fills up with the light of Allah!

Fill this heart below with as many things as you can think of that makes a person have great character!

For example, being nice to people.

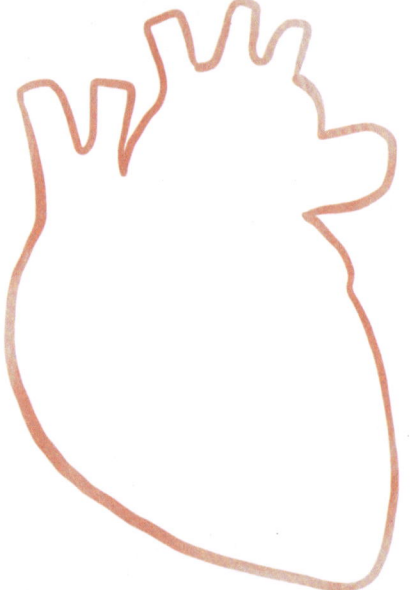

Did you know? If you recite Surah Yaseen, Allah gives you the same reward as reciting the whole Qur'an! How awesome is that!

RAMADAN DAY 23

Date : ....

Salah

- Fajr
- Dhuhr
- Asr
- Maghrib
- Isha
- Extra Prayers

Fasting

- 1/4 Fast
- 1/2 Fast
- 3/4 Fast
- Full Fast!

Worship

- ☐ I read or learned Qur'an today
- ☐ I did a good deed on the kindness chart
- ☐ ....

How was your day?

Day 24 Activity: Halal Food
24th Juz of The Qur'an

Do you love animals? Well, in the 24th Juz of the Qur'an, Allah talks about animals! He tells us about the animals that he has provided for us to eat! When they are ready for us to eat, they are prepared with Allah's name being mentioned. We then buy them at the shops that sell Halal meat.

Circle the animals that are halal for us to eat after going through this process. Remember, we cannot eat animals that eat meat.

RAMADAN DAY 24

Date : ....

Salah

| Fajr | Dhuhr | Asr | Maghrib | Isha | Extra Prayers |

Fasting

- 1/4 Fast
- 1/2 Fast
- 3/4 Fast
- Full Fast!

Worship

- ☐ I read or learned Qur'an today
- ☐ I did a good deed on the kindness chart
- ☐ ....

How was your day?

 ☐  ☐  ☐

Day 25 Activity: Heaven
25th Juz of The Qur'an

In the 25th Juz of the Qur'an, Allah gives us a description of heaven. Heaven is the place that you will go to once you leave this world if you always have the best behaviour, Insha'Allah. It's the most beautiful place in the whole universe and it's filled with lots of yummy treats! Allah tells us, the people of heaven will ask for every type of fruit they desire and it will be given to them.

In fact, anything we ask from Allah in heaven will be given to us!

Can you write down what you would ask Allah for in heaven? You can even ask for your friends and family!

RAMADAN DAY 25

Date : ....

Salah

| Fajr | Dhuhr | Asr | Maghrib | Isha | Extra Prayers |

Fasting

- 1/4 Fast
- 1/2 Fast
- 3/4 Fast
- Full Fast!

Worship

- [ ] I read or learned Qur'an today
- [ ] I did a good deed on the kindness chart
- [ ] ....

....

How was your day?

Day 26 Activity: Kindness
26th Juz of The Qur'an

My fellow Ramadan traveller, how many times do we all forget to be nice to our parents? In the 26th Juz of the Qur'an, Allah tells us to show kindness to our parents and to the people who care for us. We should always make du'a for our parents and carers, and respect them. They have been gifted to us by Allah.

Can you write down as many things as you can think of that your parents or carers have done for you?

If you are struggling, then go and ask them and I'm sure they will help you out!

_____   _____

_____   _____

_____   _____

_____   _____

_____   _____

_____   _____

Now, either make them a card or write a letter to show them how much you appreciate everything they have done for you.

RAMADAN DAY 26

Date : ....

Salah

| Fajr | Dhuhr | Asr | Maghrib | Isha | Extra Prayers |

Fasting

- 1/4 Fast
- 1/2 Fast
- 3/4 Fast
- Full Fast!

Worship

- ☐ I read or learned Qur'an today
- ☐ I did a good deed on the kindness chart
- ☐ ....

How was your day?

Day 27 Activity: Mercy
27th Juz of The Qur'an

Do you know what mercy means? It means when we forgive someone after they harm us and continue to treat them in a gentle manner. One of the names of Allah is Ar-Rahman, which means He is the most merciful ever! Wow! That means, He can forgive our mistakes if we are really sorry for doing them and strive to not do them again! Allah is so merciful that even one of the chapters in the Qur'an is called Ar-Rahman.

Here's a special activity for you today! Can you find my name, Qamar, in the verses below? You might need some help on this one!

يَخرُجُ مِنهُمَا اللُّؤْلُؤُ وَالمَرجانُ

―――――――――――――

الشَّمسُ وَالقَمَرُ بِحُسبانٍ

―――――――――――――

وَلَهُ الجَوارِ المُنشَآتُ فِي البَحرِ كَالأَعلامِ

Once you find my name, with the help of someone at home, research and write down what the arabic of each of these verses means. You may want to use an English Qur'an!

RAMADAN DAY 27

Date : ....

Salah

- Fajr
- Dhuhr
- Asr
- Maghrib
- Isha
- Extra Prayers

Fasting

- 1/4 Fast
- 1/2 Fast
- 3/4 Fast
- Full Fast!

Worship

- I read or learned Qur'an today ☐
- I did a good deed on the kindness chart ☐
- .... ☐

How was your day?

Day 28 Activity: Allah's Names
28th Juz of The Qur'an

Little travellers, you have a name and I have a name too, which is Qamar. But, do you know how many names Allah has? He has more than 99 names! Wow that is incredible. Each of these names describe something amazing about Allah. In the 28th Juz of the Qur'an, we find a lot of names of Allah written in the Qur'an.
Here are some that are mentioned in the 28th Juz of the Qur'an.

AR-RAHMAAN   Al-MALIK   AS-SALAM
AL-MUQTADIR
AL-KHAALIQ   AL-JALEEL   AL-HAKEEM

Choose three of these names from above and write down their meaning below. You may need to ask around or research online to help you.

_____

_____

_____

_____

_____

RAMADAN DAY 28

Date : ....

Salah

Fajr | Dhuhr | Asr | Maghrib | Isha | Extra Prayers

Fasting

- 1/4 Fast
- 1/2 Fast
- 3/4 Fast
- Full Fast!

Worship

- ☐ I read or learned Qur'an today
- ☐ I did a good deed on the kindness chart
- ☐ ....
- ....

How was your day?

Day 29 Activity: Our Body
29th Juz of The Qur'an

'Heads, shoulders, knees and toes, knees and toes!' You've heard this song right? Well, in the 29th Juz of the Qur'an, Allah tells us about the body parts He has given us so that we can use them to remember and worship him!

Allah tells us that he has given us ears to hear with, eyes to see with, and organs in our body. How often do we thank him for this?

Close your eyes, write down three things you can hear.

....

Open your eyes, write down three things you can see.

....

Think of three organs in your body, what do these organs do to help our body?

....

Look at your answers, raise your hands and thank Allah for giving us these gifts.

Did you know? 80% of all your learning comes from seeing.

RAMADAN DAY 29

Date : ....

Salah

| Fajr | Dhuhr | Asr | Maghrib | Isha | Extra Prayers |

Fasting

- 1/4 Fast
- 1/2 Fast
- 3/4 Fast
- Full Fast!

Worship

- [ ] I read or learned Qur'an today
- [ ] I did a good deed on the kindness chart
- [ ] ....

....

How was your day?

Day 30 Activity: Night of Power
30th Juz of The Qur'an

It's the last activity! In the last and final Juz of the Qur'an, Allah tells us about the most important and most powerful night in Ramadan called the 'Night of Power'. It may have already passed by the time you've reached this activity!

Allah tells us the following verses in the Qur'an which are written below.

1. We sent it down on the <u>Night</u> of Decree.
2. But what will convey to you what the Night of <u>Decree</u> is?
3. The Night of Decree is better than a <u>thousand</u> months.
4. In it descend the <u>angels</u> and the Spirit, by the leave of their Lord, with every command.
5. <u>Peace</u> it is; until the rise of <u>dawn</u>.

Complete the table by choosing the correct underlined words from the verse above and match it to the arabic words below.

Arabic	Meaning
Alf	
Salaam	
Layl	
Malikaah	
Qadr	
Fajr	

RAMADAN DAY 30

Date : ....

Salah

- Fajr
- Dhuhr
- Asr
- Maghrib
- Isha
- Extra Prayers

Fasting

- 1/4 Fast
- 1/2 Fast
- 3/4 Fast
- Full Fast!

Worship

- [ ] I read or learned Qur'an today
- [ ] I did a good deed on the kindness chart
- [ ] ....
  ....

How was your day?

Stage 4
Ramadan Achievements & Celebrating Eid

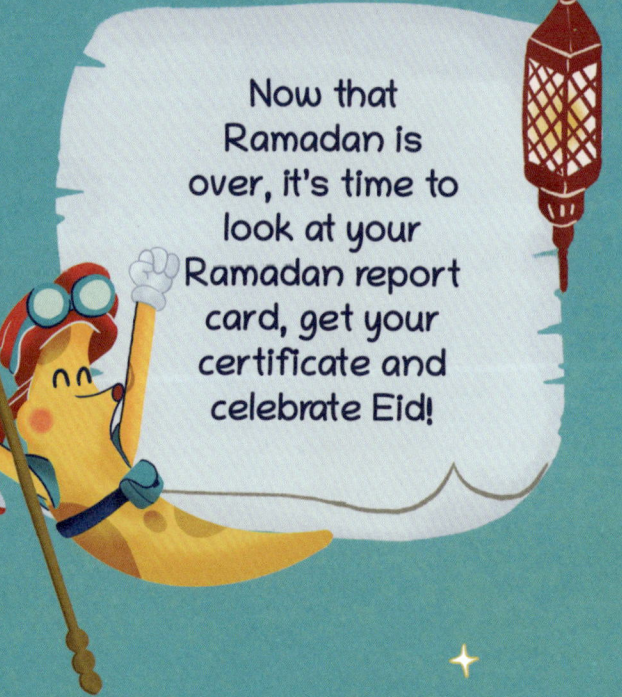

Now that Ramadan is over, it's time to look at your Ramadan report card, get your certificate and celebrate Eid!

Masha'Allah, my fellow Ramadan traveller, we've come to the end of Ramadan!

Congratulations on collecting all of the knowledge coins and doing as many good deeds as you can!

It's now time to look at how well you did in Ramadan and reflect on your Ramadan experience.

It's also time for Eid! Eid is my most favourite day of the year because I get to shine brightly in the sky as much as I can and bring happiness and joy to everyone!

Ramadan Report Card

Looking back at our progress to how many good deeds we have done is a part of our faith. Ask someone at home to help you complete your Ramadan report card below!

Number of Knowledge Coins Collected This is the number of daily activities you completed!	
Number of Fasts Completed	
Number of Prayers Completed	
Number of Kindness Chart Deeds Completed	
How Much Qur'an Did You Read or Learn?	

Masha'Allah! Congratulations and a big high five for helping me collect my missing knowledge coins! I should have enough now to go into the sky to tell everyone it is Eid time!

End of Ramadan
Reflection Page

Alhamdulillah, Ramadan has been so much fun with you! Let's reflect on our journey by writing in the spaces below.

What have you learnt?

....

What did you enjoy doing the most?

....

What did you least enjoy?

....

What good deeds will you continue doing after Ramadan?

....

What bad deeds will you stop doing after Ramadan?

....

How can you make next Ramadan even better?

....

Certificate

MY LITTLE RAMADAN LEGACY CERTIFICATE OF ACHIEVEMENT

Awarded to

_____

for being patient and super awesome in successfully completing My Little Legacy Ramadan Journal & for worshipping Allah and showing Him the best I can be!

_____
Signed by Parent/Guardian

Celebrating Eid

We celebrate the end of Ramadan with Eid-Ul-Fitr. Eid is announced when the new moon is spotted in the sky. That's me Qamar! Let's see if you can spot me in the sky again on the night of Eid :)

On this super awesome and fun day, Muslims around the world prepare for Eid in the best way possible!

1. Taking a shower before Eid prayer
2. Put on some awesome clothes!
3. Eat something yummy before Eid prayer like some dates!
4. Recite the Eid Takbeerat on the next page!
5. Pray the Eid prayer

- Visit your family
- Decorate your house
- Make cards
- Say Eid greeting to family and family
- Apply Henna (for females)

Eid Morning Takbeerat

اللَّهُ أَكْبَرُ اللَّهُ أَكْبَرُ
لَا إِلَهَ إِلَّا اللَّهُ وَاللَّهُ أَكْبَرُ
اللَّهُ أَكْبَرُ وَلِلَّهِ الْحَمْدْ

Allahu Akbar, Allahu Akbar,
La Ilaha Ilallahu Wallahu Akbar,
Allahu Akbar, Wa Lillahil Hamd.

It's Eid Day!

Draw or stick a picture of your Eid celebration day!

Write about how your day was. What did you enjoy the most? What kind of foods did you eat? Who did you visit? How many people did you say "Eid mubarak" to?

....

....

....

Remember my fellow travellers, every year I will need your help collecting even more missing knowledge coins. In fact there aren't only just 30 knowledge coins in the world but there are millions and millions! Now that Ramadan is over, I pray to Allah that you always collect knowledge throughout your whole life and I hope you stay happy, warm and super awesome! Always remember Allah, your fasting, your prayers and all the good deeds to do in your life :)

Until next time!
Your Moon Qamar

Answer Sheet for My Little Legacy: Ramadan Kids Journal & Activity Book

Riddles

I was revealed in the month of Ramadan. Leave me and you will never find the treasure of happiness. I come in the form of words or the shape of a book. What am I? Quran

I am the fourth pillar of Islam. I come once a year. I arrive and leave depending on the moon. What am I? Sawm

I am an important meal when the fast comes to an end, but not when the fast begins. What am I? Iftar

I am the night in which the Qur'an was sent down. I am better than a thousand years. What am I? Laylatul Qadr

Some people wake up for me and some people dont, but our Prophet Muhammad (peace be upon him) said to have me, because there is blessing in me. What am I? Suhoor

I come in different forms. I could be money or time. If these are not possible, I can simply be a smile. What am I? Charity

I arrive at different times during the day. I don't stay for long, so catch me at my given times or you will lose the rewards that come from me. Salah

Answers for Activity Pages

Activity 1: Gratitude

This is an open ended activity. Start your child off by asking them to look around them at things they can physically see that are blessings from Allah swt. Then, ask them to think about things outside of their home that is a blessing from Allah swt. Finally, to encourage deeper thinking, ask them what kind of things has Allah blessed us with that we can not see.

Activity 2: Fasting

Please note the answers for this activity can vary. Here are some important rules about fasting:
1. Muslims who are fasting must not eat or drink from sunrise to sunset.
2. Muslims should not get angry or engage in fowl language.
3. Accidently eating or drinking does not break your fast.
4. If you are travelling or sick in Ramadan, you don't need to fast but must make it up later.
5. If you are old and sick and can not fast, you must give fidiya, that is, feeding a person for each day of the missed fasts.

Activity 3: Protection

Remind your children that the ultimate protection comes from Allah swt and this can be achieved by reciting Ayat al-Kursi. Encourage them to memorise this verse, you could write down one line for them and give them three days to memorise each line. Of course how much time you give them depends on their age. The older they are, the less time it should take them to memorise. Reward them when they have learnt it.

Activity 4: Du'a

Encouraging your children to make du'a from a young age is really important. When your child asks you for something specific, eg. Ipad, new toy, you could simply ask them to make du'a and ask Allah swt that if it is good for you then may he grant it to you and if it is bad for you then keep it away from you. Ultimately, your child will develop the understanding that Allah swt is Ar-Razzaaq, the provider.

Activity 5: Fairness

Teaching your children to be fair at all times is very important. Being Just is one of the central ideas of the Quran. Also, it is one of the most important attributes of Allah swt, Al-Muqsit, the just one.

Answers:
Musa playing with play dough........Unfair
Fatima is riding a bike..................Unfair
Yahya was having a party.............Fair

Activity 6: Wudu

Step 1
Start with Bismillah
Step 2
Wash both your hands up to the wrists three times

Step 3
Rinse your mouth three times
Step 4
Rinse your nose three times
Step 5
Wash your face three times
Step 6
Wash both arms up to the elbow three times.
Step 7
Wash over the head, behind and inside the ears
Step 8
Wash both feet up to the ankles three times.

Activity 7: Miracles

Miracles performed by Isa (as)
He blew into clay birds and they started to fly
He made the sick better
He cured the blind
He spoke as a baby to protect his mother

Miracles by Musa (as)
He split the red sea

Activity 8: The Creation

Allah created Adam and ordered the angels to bow down to him. Iblis did not bow down to Adam. Iblis became a disbeliever and promised to trick people. Allah then created Hawa and told her and Adam to eat the fruits around them, except from one tree. Iblis tricked them. He told them if they eat from the forbidden tree they would live forever. Adam and Hawa disobeyed Allah by eating from that tree. Allah sent them out of Jannah to live on Earth.
Adam and Hawa cried so much and kept asking Allah for forgiveness. Because Allah is Merciful and forgiving, He forgave them.

The names of Adam (as) first two son's are Habil and Qabil.

Activity 9: Patience

This activity will require your child to really think back to a time they showed patience. Allow them to think about and talk to you about it first. You can help guide them with this activity by prompting them, for example, Can you remember a time you were waiting for a specific gift? Have you had to wait in a long queue? Or you could discuss a time someone said something hurtful to them and they showed patience by not saying harsh words back.

Ask your children what they would ask Allah to make these times easier. Will they ask Allah to grant them beautiful patience, like the advice given by Yaqoub (as) to his son Yusuf (as).

Activity 10: Islamic Months

Muharram; Safar; Rabi' ul-awwal; Rabi' al-thani; Jumada al-awwal; Jumādā al-Thānī, Rajab; Sha'ban; Ramadan;Shawwal; Dhul-Qi'dah, Dhū al-Hijjah

Four sacred months are:
Muharram - this is the first month of the Islamic new year and ashura is on the 10th day of this month.

Rabi ul awwal - This is the month where the prophet (saw) made the night journey from the kaaba to Al aqsa and then to the heavens.

Dhul - Qi'dah - This is the eleventh month of the islamic calendar and comes before the month of hajj.

Dhul hijjah - this is the month where muslims do hajj and celebrate Eid ul Adha.

Activity 11: Mistakes

6. A whale swallows prophet Yunus, where he reads a dua for forgiveness.
4. Yunus (as) sets sail on a boat
7. The people of Nineveh are really happy to see Yunus (as) again.
1. Yunus (as) tells the people to believe in Allah alone.
5. A storm happens and Yunus (as)'s name comes up to jump into the sea
3. Yunus (as) left his people in anger
2. The people of Nineveh reject his call to worship Allah only.

The dua Yunus (as) made in the belly of the whale was:

La ilaha illa anta, Subhanaka, Inni kuntu minaz-zalimin

Activity 12: Yusuf

Four facts can be anything from the whole story, here are some:
- Yusuf (as) tells his dream to his father Yaqub (as)

- Yusuf (as) father tells him not to tell his brothers the dream because they may get jealous.
- Yusufs (as) brothers are jealous of him and his brother binyamin (as)n and plot to kill Yusuf.
- The brothers take Yusuf out with their fathers permission and throw Yusuf (as) into a well.
- Some travellers passing by find Yusuf (as) in the well
- Yusuf's brothers tell their father that Yusuf was eaten by a wolf.

Activity 13: Allah's Help

Why did the people around Prophet Ibrahim pray to idols?
They fell for Shaytan's trick.

Prophet Ibrahim had a plan to get rid of the idols and so when the people around him left, what did he do to the idols?
He smashed all of the idols with his strength.

Why did the people around Prophet Ibrahim want to hurt him?
They thought he was a danger to how they wanted to live.

The people around Prophet Ibrahim threw him into a fire, why did the fire not hurt him?
Allah told the fire to be cool for him.

Why do you think Allah helped the Prophet Ibrahim when he was thrown into a fire?
Listen to the reasons the child comes up with based on their knowledge of the story of Ibrahim (as).

Activity 14: Nature

This is a fun activity for the children to enjoy whilst learning about the amazing nature of bees. You could challenge them further by asking them to find these fruits mentioned in the Quran.

Activity 15: Insha'Allah

The startments where inshallah can be said are:
I am going to build a cardboard mosque inshallah
I will go to my grandparents house next week inshallah
Tomorrow, I will recite quran inshallah
I will pray all my salahs today, inshallah

Activity 16: Provisions

The tree with the dates is in the bottom right hand corner.
Some of the benefits of eating dates are: They provide a natural source of energy and minerals such as potassium.

Activity 17: Hajj

Have lots of fun doing this! Allow the children to explore the shape of a cube and think about how they can construct it. Why not take it a step further, paint it and create the rest of the masjid using paper and card. Share your ideas with us here! We would love to see them!

Ibrahim (as) built the ka'bah.

Activity 18: Nuh (as)

Can you think of a time when you helped or saved someone else from being hurt?
Encourage the child to think about how they have helped others from being hurt? It could be from being bullied or falling down whilst playing.

Activity 19: Musa

Can you think of a time when someone has saved you from a difficult situation?
This question is open to answers depending on your child. This could even be a time where your child was finding it difficult to calculate a math question and received help from a friend.

Activity 20: Allah's Protection

Can you think of a time when someone had protected you. What did they do and did you say thank you to them?
This is also open to answers. You can prompt the child to talk about a parent or carer protecting them.

Activity 21: Praying

This activity teaches your child to tell the time, especially for salah. It would be a fun way to get the children to be alert of what the clock looks like at the exact time for each salah. Younger children will find this task tricky, you can help them by using a real clock and setting the times manually for each salah so that they can copy it into their journal.

Activity 22: Nature

There are many different types of fish that can be included here. I have given some here, but there are many more for you to find. Send us your drawings, we would love to see all the different types of fish you have drawn.

Freshwater Fish:
Catfish
Trout
Bass

Saltwater Fish:
Tuna
Cod
Mackerel
Shark

Activity 23: The Heart

Being polite
Saying please and thank you
Being patient
Listening to your parents
Helping others

Activity 24: Halal Food

Cow, goat, camel, chicken, rabbit and sheep

Activity 25: Heaven

This activity encourages your child to think about jannah as the ultimate goal. Talking to them about what they would ask Allah for in heaven, helps them to understand and visualise the beautiful dwelling place. Please share some of these with us on our page!

Activity 26: Kindness

I'm sure you will love to see what the children come up with for this one! If they come to you for help, don't give them the answer straight away. Instead, ask them to think about their day to day life and where during the day do mums, dads or carers help them. Please share any letters or cards your children make for you with us.

Activity 27: Mercy

The word Qamar is the second word on the second line.

The translation of these ayas are:

يَخْرُجُ مِنْهُمَا اللُّؤْلُؤُ وَالْمَرْجَانُ
From both of them emerge pearl and coral

الشَّمْسُ وَالْقَمَرُ بِحُسْبَانٍ
The sun and the moon for reckoning

وَلَهُ الْجَوَارِ الْمُنْشَآتُ فِي الْبَحْرِ كَالْأَعْلَامِ
And to him belong the ships (with sails) elevated in the sea like mountains

Activity 28: Allah's Names

Ar-Rahman - The Most Merciful
Al-Malik - The King
As-Salam - The Source of Peace
Al-Muqtadir - The Determiner
Al - Khaaliq - The Creator
Al - Jaleel - The Mighty
Al - Hakeem - The Wise

Activity 29: Our body

This activity helps your child to understand some of the beautiful gifts from Allah swt that we don't always remember to thank him for. This is an open ended activity and the answers will vary. Why not take this activity a step further! Blind fold your child and then give them simple tasks to do such as bringing you something from another room. They will most probably take a while to do this. This is an excellent way to teach them how powerful the gift of sight is from Allah and that we should make du'a for those who have lost their sight. (This activity can be done with hearing and speech as well).

Activity 30: Night of Power

Alf - thousand
Salaam - Peace
Layl - Night
Malikaah - Angels

Qadr - Decree
Fajr - dawn